MAKING I   ESTATE SALES

OUR GUIDE TO STARTING AND GROWING A SUCCESSFUL ESTATE SALE BUSINESS

WE WELCOME ALL ASPIRING ESTATE SALES PEOPLE WHO NEED A LITTLE HELP IN GROWING INTO A LARGER BUSINESS THROUGH USING THIS BOOK

MARGARET A. ANGELL–EVANS
AND W. DIEHL EVANS
OWNERS OF
ANGELL ESTATE SALES & APPRAISAL SERVICES, INC.

MAKING MONEY WITH ESTATE SALES

OUR GUIDE TO STARTING AND GROWING A SUCCESSFUL ESTATE SALE BUSINESS

BY

DIEHL EVANS

www.bookstandpublishing.com

Published by
Bookstand Publishing
Morgan Hill, CA 95037
3605_3

ISBN 978-1-61863-199-2

Printed in the United States of America

FOREWORD

One of our greatest joys is when all of our workers meet together at a local restaurant after the sale to share their experiences. This is why we call them our second family.

We have certainly enjoyed the people who have worked for us and more with us than for us. They are like a family and many have become qualified in pricing and a great help in putting an estate sale together. Some of the photographs in the book show them doing their special jobs. Then we also have others who work in the sales as well as help in putting an estate sale together. Some work as cashiers while others work as sales people.

Some have retired and come by to visit as we are putting a sale together. A few have become restricted to what they can do while others couldn't come back due to family conditions.

We still love them all and this book is dedicated to all in the past as well as now and in the future.

ACKNOWLEDGEMENTS

We wish to express our gratitude to those who helped us with their encouragement in the publishing of this book, especially to Clark & Leslie Angell.

To our Doctors Joel C. Silverfield & W. B. Edgerton Jr. MD. who keep us in good health.

To King Printing for their advice and knowledge.

To our workers who supplied us with funny stories that are in this book.

To all the different moving companies that have moved many tons of furniture in our sales.

To Legal Zoom who helped us get our copyright registered with the Library of Congress.

We especially appreciate R. Palmer Angell, Jr., for his assistance and knowledge in putting together all of our estate sales.

TABLE OF CONTENTS

CHAPTER 1

ESTATE SALES, WHERE AND WHEN

Questions I often ask me, why do you want to do estate sales? Well I suppose it is a good way to help people settle their estate problems. Or it is a place to get rid of stuff that folks do not need anymore. You know, turn stuff into cash, so they can buy something else.

Newly Weds, tell us they have out fitted their house or apartment with stuff from our estate sales. They said it helped stretch their budget by buying second hand things.

I guess it is also like a treasure hunt, you never know what you will find in the bottom of an old trunk or up in an attic. Under all that dust on an oil painting is a long lost Van Gogh or a Rembrandt, it could be a real "Blue Boy".

Yes, it is all the above and more, whether it is a small tag sale or a large auction, the thrill is always there. The thrill is always in the hunt and especially if you made a good deal.

Estate sales are generally held over a two-day period. Some use a Friday - Saturday while others are held on a Saturday - Sunday approach. A lot would depend on how much stuff you would have to sell or auction, the size of the place you will need to have and customer parking

The day before our sales we put signs on street comers directing to the location where the sale will be held. This is done in the late evening and you need to be careful because if you put your sign on someone's property without their permission it will probably be missing the next day. We had an occasion where, after putting out some direction signs we went back to the Estate Sale house to find two cars parked in the driveway. They were waiting for us to open up the sale. That's pretty fast action for signs even if it was a day early. It pays to advertise!!

One of our sales had a chain link fence around the property, a fairly large house about 3500 square feet and a five-acre lot in front. We lined the lot into rows for parking and locked the gate on the entrance. A newspaper reporter was doing a story on the buyers and why they would stand in line. The reporter asked us how early he should come to interview some of the buyers. We told him they probably would line up about 5:00

1

am. He brought his photographer and they had a field day interviewing our customers. Some of the crowd was being upset when a car pulled into the driveway and pulled up to the gate. We had an off duty Deputy there that was opening the gate for some customers to get inside. The person in the car jumped the gun and drove the car into the open gate he hollered stop and she stopped with one tire on top of the Deputy's foot. He said later that he would give her a piece of his mind and he looked up and saw some people from-his church, biting his tongue he asked her to back up off his foot. She backed up, he removed his foot, and she took off down the driveway. The Deputy told me it was a good idea that he wore hi steel-toed boots.

That house had some real problems; after being vacant for two years; the plumbing had backed up in the drain field. We ordered four "Port O Pots" to be delivered the day before our sale and they were late getting to us. In this business, you have to be prepared for anything. 1.

Some estates are very large, like a multi millionaire, or a very famous person with a varied collection, like Mr. Du Pont who had a collection so large that it became a museum. It covers a huge area, thousands and thousands of wonderful antiques. So large it would take the combined efforts of the largest auction companies and considerable time to catalog and price the items. You say why would they put prices on things that they are going to auction. Good question, all good auction companies consider the price that an item will fetch when put on the block, it's just good business to make an estimate and this is usually put in their catalog to give potential buyers a value before the auction. The idea here is simple; the large amount of items to sell will require a lot of time to put a sale together and a considerable amount of money. The knowledge of all the items as to age, condition, quality, identification and authenticate, would require a number of qualified appraisers to handle the job.

So we hope you do not plan to start up your estate sales business that large or maybe you might start a little smaller, well we know how to help you with that too. Let us start with a small two-bedroom house, no antiques, just furniture and stuff.

The stuff is garage sale type of things. Your help is you, yourself and no one else. The biggest part of this kind of job is to get rid of the accumulation of trash and clean the place up. The owners of the estate expect you to liquidate their things and stuff into money. So grab a broom and many trash bags and get started.

Now you have the garage cleaned out and you have set card tables up in rows. From the house you take the garage sale items and arrange them into categories' like pots & pans knick-knacks and so on. Next, you want to rearrange the furniture in the house, bring the dining room chairs out of the bedroom and place them in the dining area. Check the flatware and dishes, if they are dirty and dull, wash and polish them. Silverware that is polished will sell a lot quicker. Polish the furniture and clean the floors. All things are now ready to sell. No" What about prices! Ok, let us take it one-step at a time, you have been to garage sales and you know how to handle those items. Now furniture and appliances, if you do not know how to price these items, get your pad and pencil, make a visit to your neighborhood Goodwill store and used furniture stores. Think of the condition of your sofa, the chairs, tables, etc and make note of their prices. Remember you plan to have a two-day sale, right; you want to sell everything, right. Those stores plan to sell their things over a much longer period. Even if your stuff is in better condition, you still must reduce your prices below theirs. It may take you several sales to get your prices right. We also have a little trick that we use ourselves, if you have a prospect who is interested in, let's say the sofa, hand them a card, which we call a bid card, (see.-example) and tell them to make a bid and you will call them later after you close if they have a successful bid.

Sometimes, you have a small estate in a small house and it would require a minimum number of workers. The biggest part of this kind of job is to get rid of the accumulation of trash and clean the place up.

We were asked to liquidate an estate that was in a small, two-bedroom house. We worked for three weeks carrying bags of old receipts, bills, papers, etc., after about thirty trash bags full we were able to see the floors and discovered how dirty it was. Yes, it is hard work. If you have ever moved yourself, you have a good idea about cleaning *out a* house to make it ready for a sale.

Another estate, the deceased owner had been a compulsive buyer. We thought it strange when we saw a telephone on the outside of a window ledge until we tried to go in the front door. Wall to wall and floor to ceiling was stuff that was bought and still in its original boxes. We had to take boxes *out* to make a pathway to go in. The owner had been sleeping in a small portable storage unit near the telephone. Now that was a compulsive buyer. Another compulsive buyer asked permission to bring some things to an estate sale we were getting ready, we said sure brings it to us. When a large semi - trailer backed up our driveway and started to unload box after box of Tupper ware, household appliances, and other sundry items. The three-car garage was so full we had to stack the Tupperware outside.

CHAPTER 2

HOW TO PRICE

Pricing residential contents is usually done in three ways. One is over pricing, two is pricing to low and three is pricing at Fair Market Value. Certainly, you do not want number one, because you will not sell very many items and number two is priced too low which means you would not make much money for your client and your commission would be less.

What do we mean by Fair Market Value? Fair Market Value is the most probable price at which property would change hands between a willing buyer and a willing seller, neither being under any compulsion to buy or sell both having reasonable knowledge of all relevant facts and with the sale being made to the public in the most relevant market taking into consideration the location of the property.

This also would mean that proper advertising must be done in advance of a sale. This would not be a forced liquidation value, which is the most probable price for which an item would change hands if sold immediately without regard to the best market. In addition, there is little time to find an open market and advertise properly since the property is being under compulsion to sell.

Is there a book that gives you prices for things and stuff? No there is no such books! These prices are similar to prices you would expect at an auction or an estate sale. They are not retail prices that you would find in an antique and collectable pricing guide.

how do you start? Visit many second hand furniture stores, become familiar with their prices. Attend many auctions who auction household items. Also, go to many estate sales and observe their prices on things. Become familiar with retail store pricing and their special sales prices.

Who made the furniture, which is very important? For example, a veneer over -pressed wood looks nice but it costs less to manufacture. On the other hand top of the line furniture companies use the best grades of wood and materials and their prices would reflect good quality. So be careful when you compare prices of poorly made furniture to the top of the line furniture.

It is comparable to prices in antique pricing guides. However, keep in mind those are for retail sales, your prices will be below that unless the item is a rare piece and its quality and condition are excellent. Then you must consider the area that your sale will be held. Will this item be in any demand? If not you must consider prices to fit the area. Simple economics, it is important that things will sell well in high-end neighborhoods.

It will take time for you to be able to identify antiques; even then, it will take more time to be able to know if it is a good piece or a reproduction. There are a lot of copies and reproductions in the world market place of antiques. Everything of good and great value is subject to be copied by unscrupulous people.

You will hear comments such as; my grandmother gave it to me. The grandmother is in her sixties and the granddaughter is in her twenties. That makes the item forty years old.

However, to the inexperienced person even forty years seems like a long enough time to call something an antique. However, the museums and historians consider that an item must have been made prior to 1840. Today many antique dealers consider that all items over 100 years old are an antique. The televised "Road Show" has very good appraisers who have done a great job explaining the concept of what is still considered a true antique.

Most dealers in antiques cover this questionable area with the term collectables and many Pricing Guide books are calling their books "Antiques and Collectables".

Therefore, your education on antiques is going to require a lot of "due diligence" on your part to become familiar with antiques. There are many fine books on the subject of antiques. Attend antique shows and shops. Antiques come in a great variety of items like jewelry, glass, china, wood, metal, all kinds of furniture and many more.

We have been doing estate sales over 30 years and we are still learning about antiques.

During this time, we have taken courses with Sotheby's in London, Winterthur Museum in Delaware, MESDA (Museum of Early Southern Decorative Art) in Winston Salem, North Carolina, Caen University in Normandy, France. We have sold antiques in a shop and have been an Antique Show Dealer. The most important thing is to keep learning throughout your life, you will never learn too much.

Do not be afraid to ask questions or seek knowledge. Sometimes it is a lot like being a detective where one bit of information leads to another step in being able to identity and price at fair market value.

Find people in your area who are qualified appraisers, get to know them, find out their specialties in antiques, use them, they may charge you a fee but it will be worth it to have the right prices.

We have used one appraiser who is very qualified for oriental items and provides us with correct prices.

Our library is in our office and one wall is covered with bookcases filled with books on everything imaginable. There are books on antiques, appraisals, baseball items, china, carpets both antique and modem, auction house prices, silver, glass, and so much more, it would take the place of our book. However, you do not have to have an extensive library, because you have a public library in your town or nearby that, you can use.

Use the internet to find things. I needed to verify a gun maker in London, England, so I used Google, asked for a street directory for Fleet Street, London, England, and dated 1795. I got it in seconds and found my gun maker at the right address.

You cannot know everything but you do need to know where to go to find that information.

China! Ceramics

Many estates have older pieces of ceramics or china handed down from several generations in almost any part of our country. Especially in retirement, areas where empty nest couples are downsizing their things and stuff and not much room in their new abodes for unnecessary stuff if you are in any such areas do not be surprised if you are asked to sell some older pieces of china!

The most common are Chinese Export and Japanese Export. If you are knowledgeable about this field of ceramics, please excuse us, for we do not want to fill up the page with a lot of idle chitchat.

If you are not familiar with this area of your expertise, we hope this will help you in your efforts to put together a great sale after another great sale. To start with, our advice is to make a list of qualified personal property appraisers in your area and get to know them and their specialties, because you cannot know everything about all things.

So let us start with the info.

Canton China is blue and white porcelain that was very popular back in the 17th Century and 18th Century. More than 60 million pieces of Chinese porcelain were sent to the West before 1800. That means a lot of that stuff is still lying around and many collectors want it.

However, you must know how to recognize a piece when you *see* one. What do they look like? Well, there may be a plate, bowl, platter, charger, vases. Some are dishes and some are dishes with covers.

A common pattern is on the example page. You can buy a pricing guide but do not expect to get their price because that's a price used as retail.

By 1840, blue and white ceramics coming from China were called Canton or ballast ware.

Sailing ships used crates of this porcelain in the ships hold for ballast and after landing at New York, Boston, or Charleston they would sell their ballast for a handsome profit.

Nevertheless, not all-Chinese export is blue and white, it comes in several colors, when one color is used it's called monochrome and when multiple colors are used it's called polychrome.

In the early Ming Dynasty their colors, were enamels of brown, green, purple, yellow and red-orange.

EXHIBITS

Jardinière, 15" diameter, 12" high
Chinese circa-1796-1820.
Sold for $600

Notice the side panel that is enlarged and the clothes on the characters. It looks like some that was worn in the 1700's. The Chinese were trying to give the porcelain a look of the west, as they imagined us, adults playing with children.

EXHIBITS

Punch Bowl
Chinese Famille Rose, 14" diameter, 7"high. Sometimes called "Rose Medallion." Made in T'ung-Chih period, circa-1862-1874 A.D. Sold for $500.00

Rose Mandarin is a pattern of Chinese export porcelain decorated in rose pink colors. The Mandarin is seated behind a table and watching a comic or court Jester performing with some women. The Plate is 12" in diameter, circa-1885-1900 Sold for $250.00

EXHIBITS

Jardinière in the Rose Medallion pattern of Chinese export, 12" high x 14" diameter. Sold for $120.00 Circa 1920's.

Large Jar with cover, 19" high, note gold Foo dog on cover, famille verte in an under glaze of blue with decorations of green. sold for $600.00 circa-1862-1874 A.D.

EXHIBITS

Canton Blue & White Export Ware

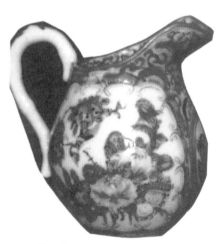

Cloisonné   **Famille Rose Export Ware**

In the early 1700's the merchants demand introduced new colors that changed Chinese porcelain forever.

The new colors were white and pink and became the preferred colors that pink could be shaded to alter the pink and this new way was called palettes with a combination of enamels. These palettes were called Famille or (family), Verte, Noire, Jaune and Rose. The Verte palette is composed of green, yellow, aubergine, orange and blue. The noire palette was used normally on a black background. The jaune palette used Famille rose colors with a yellow background. The rose Famille palette added shades of pink predomination over green.

We only mention these palettes because a graduation of color, translucency, and position of colors are used as dating tools and these changes were made over time and were recorded. With these many colors with gold added, the porcelain became beautiful and very desirable. Famille Rose, Rose Mandarin, and Rose Medallion patterns were made for export. Many other styles were made as China copied Japanese Imari to compete with Japanese Export trade.

A reproduction Alert! America has been flooded with modem Chinese reproductions.

They are not ceramics but stoneware, and not translucent to light. Japanese Imari is still very collectable, decorated in red. Sometimes gold on a white ground, with the use of green, yellow, blue and black.

If you find any of these pieces in one of your sales, our advice is to seek a qualified appraiser who is familiar with oriental merchandise for authentication and pricing.

European China

Most common is the Haveland China or Limoges, which is the area of France that it is produced in, and is not as popular as it once was.

Meissen has made a lot of fine porcelain, especially in figurines and other items. Their mark is crossed swords in blue on a white ground. Prices are found in most pricing guides. There are several other makers in the Dresden part of Germany and are marked Dresden or to copy Meissen's crossed swords.

Se'vres china was in operation in1753 in Se'vres, France that was located between Paris and Versailles on the Seine River and produced very fine porcelain.

In fact, their porcelain was so good that for the first 5 years they produced items for the Royal family only. This bit of information I picked up at a ceramics class at Sotheby's in London, England.

My wife and I had enrolled in a three weeks course on the study of ceramics (or china as we on this side of the pond know it) and I have a bad habit of nodding off when the lights go out and a soft hum of the projector is heard. Well I must have been awake most of the time because we passed their test at the end of the course but that's another story.

Back to Se'vres porcelain and their mark is on exhibit page, it is a pair of script L has intertwined with a date letter in the center.

A couple of years later we were preparing an estate sale, that's like getting stuff together, my sweet wife returned from picking up stuff for the sale. She hands me a vase with lid and on its bottom was a Se'vres mark that showed a date mark of 1756. My first thought was how did this piece get out of the royal family and end up in Tampa, Florida. My second thought was this must be a well-made fake or a fraud. A copy is usually a compliment to the original but a fraud is fooling a buyer and taking his money. At our ceramics, class in London an instructor gave us several tips to prove or disprove the piece as being legitimate and made by Se'vres in 1756. First check it for basic things, did it look like same colors as early similar pieces. The colors were as close as could be determined.

Next was check for basic things like is it soft paste or hard paste porcelain. Again, our instructor told us to check for soft paste was by feel, it should feel a little soapy. She also said when she is away for a couple of weeks; she found it a lot harder to do.

Well, it occurred to me that was too hard to determine accurately. Therefore, I tried to check it for hard paste by taking a small jewelry file and make a nick in the porcelain. I selected a non-noticeable spot in the base.

A bright light on the spot reveled small bits that sparkled like mica. That showed me it was hard paste but that brought up another question.

Where did Se'vres find the clay that made hard paste porcelain? After serious checking records regarding France's geology, I found that kaolin was not found or used by potters until late 1700's or early 1800's. Therefore, my conclusion was that it must be a fake made by Samson the Imitator who was known to have copied many old pieces in the early 1800's.

England is known for Wedgwood, Royal Daulton, Spode and Royal Worchester. Spain of course has its famous LLardo figurines.

14

America has a number of good potters, Weller is getting harder to find and carries a good price tag. Rookwood also carries a good price if you can find it. McCoy and Hull are still plentiful.

Glassware is always' a good seller, like Waterford, lead crystal and cut glass. Cut glass has been slow lately due to a reproduction out of Central Europe.

Of course, you can count on Depression and Carnival glass filling in the vacant spots. Big Names like Tiffany, LaLique, and Baccarat are always excellent sellers. Peachblow is one of my favorites but watch out for copies.

EXHIBITS

Se'vres Date Marks

		1781-DD
		1782-EE
		1783-FF
1753-A	1767-0	1784-GG
1754-8	1768-P	1785-HH
1755-C	1769-Q	1786-11
1756-D	1770-R	1787-JJ
1757-E	1771-S	1788-KK
1758-F	1772-T	1789-LL
1759-G	1773-U	1790-
1760-H	1774-V	MM
1761-1	1775-X	1791-NN
1762-J	1776-Y	1792-00
1763-K	1777-Z	1793-PP
1764-L	1778-M	
1765-M	1779-88	
1766-N	1780-CC	

175
3

Soft paste

1773

Hard paste

Sterling and Silver Plate

Silver comes in two types, Silver Plate and Sterling.

Silver plate began in Sheffield, England about 1742 by Thomas Boulsover who discovered two metals when heated to a certain degree became adhered to each other. A young apprentice named Josiah Hancock who worked for Boulsover, carried on the new plating business making larger pieces. The new industry caught on by others and soon became so large that many who could not afford sterling silver sought these items.

For many years, Sheffield fostered the production of nearly all the Plate made in England. Very few pieces can be found in homes today of this early plating. Thus, the value of old silver plate found today will fetch a handsome price.

Silver Plating did not catch on in the United States until 1850's and by then an electro method and called Electro Plating or EPNS or Electro Plate Nickel Silver accomplished the process. The best way to tell old silver plate from the newer method was because the old method of rolling on a thin layer of pure silver over copper and heating the item to the adhering temperature, which left no applied borders and rims. Copper wearing through the silver plate also identified the old method. By checking the rims and edges with your fingernail, you can quickly determine the rolled process piece from the newer plated items. If you find a rolled on silver piece, check the item for a makers mark. Wyler's book on old silver carries the maker's marks on plated items.

Sterling silver in the United States will be marked sterling, which means the item has 925 parts of a 1000 of pure silver. Before 1840's the term used for old silver was marked "COIN" as silver coins were melted down to make spoons and forks for table flatware. United States coins (dimes, quarters, half dollars and dollars) have 90% sterling prior to the clad silver coins of 1965 and through present dates.

In the 17th, 18Th and I 9''' centuries all flatware and hollow ware made in the United States was made with silver coins. The Silver Smith would melt the coins and pour the molten silver into moulds. The Smith would stamp his mark on the items and include the name COIN to denote the quality of the piece. These marks will give the date made and who made the items.

About 1850 the government required that all sterling items be stamped with the mark Sterling. Today all Silver Companies mark their items this way and add their names and sometimes the pattern.

Flat ware is getting harder to sell mostly because newlyweds don't want to polish the silver pieces. If you do not polish silver it will turn black, do to oxidation with air. It does not matter if its sterling or silver plate it will all turn black.

Thus with manufactures making most of the famous patterns of sterling into stainless steel, no one wants the labor of polishing, and stainless steel is so much cheaper.

Today you can pick up a 4-piece 4-place sterling set of flatware under $500.00 at most estate sales. However great Silver companies like Gorham, Kirk Steiff, Reed & Barton, and Towle are still making Chantilly, Repousse and many other patterns.

American Silver is easy to identify because all sterling is marked sterling and all silver plate is marked EPNS (which means electric plate nickel silver) or Quadruple Plate, which means extra plate and other various terms of plating.

Hollow ware, things like bowls, trays, coffee etc. are all marked the same way as flat ware. In this category, the most desirable hollow ware is the Coffee and Tea Service with the extra pieces of cream, sugar and waste bowl. These are normally sold with a large two-handle tray. The coffee and tea service may be marked sterling but the tray is usually silver plate. Again, however, if the tray is marked sterling and all pieces match, you have a rare find and the set would bring premium prices.

Other hollow ware items that bring top dollar are sterling mint julep cups, water goblets, water pitcher, salt, and peppershakers. *We* once had a Tiffany sterling water pitcher that dealers fought over, even with a $1000.00 price tag.

Other sterling pieces are candelabras, which bring good prices.

We had appraised an estate that had a pair of English sterling seven light candelabras very heavy and not weighted on the bottom very ornate and dated 1791 by a London silversmith named Peter Bateman son of Hester Bateman, a very popular silversmith family. A research disclosed that Bateman products on auction were exceptionally high. The pair was in excellent condition and was valued at $50,000.00 for estate purposes. At auction in London, they would be worth double the estate value.

Don't forget that beautiful centerpieces are made out of silver plate and they bring a premium price.

Early American silver was made with just the maker's initials and not many people could afford fancy things, like silver. Most silver was fashioned into drinking mugs, candlesticks, and things to impress others.

As the country became more prosperous, customers demanded to know that the items of silver were not being cheated by adding lead to the silver and they were familiar with English laws on mandatory marks showing the silver quality. Some of the smiths started using pseudo touch marks and then marking them coin as they were made from silver coins.

Some marks on sterling:

England-----------------Lion Passant is the English Sterling Mark
England ----------------- Leopard's head denotes made in London Early American only had initials of the Silver Smith
United States------------Mark before 1 850's **[COIN]**
United States------------Mark after 1850"s Sterling
United States -----------Mark for Silver Plate- **EPNS** (means electro plate nickel silver)
United States -----------Mark for Silver Plate - Quadruple Plate
United States------------Mark for Silver Plate-Plated or Silver plate
Mexico------------------Sterling or 925.0
Mexico-----------------No mark probably a lower grade of silver
Italy---------------------925.0
Some European Countries ---800 & 925.0

We suggest you buy the book of OLD SILVER by Wyler; it covers Britain, Scotland, Ireland and all of Europe. Another book is Jackson's Silver and Gold Marks.

Furniture

Most furniture in today's estate sales are American made and are a mixture or blend of early styles or completely modem.

Back in this chapter we discussed the names of present day furniture makers whose products are very good furniture.

Period antiques, is a term that denotes apiece made during the original time frame of its design.

Age-Life Depreciation Guide

Insurance adjusters and moving companies use this guide to determine useful life on items and actual cash value less depreciation.

Age-Life depreciation guides do not apply to appreciable property such as antiques or collectables.

Most important is to remember this is a guide to assist you to determine a value on used furniture and appliances and is adjustable up or down depending on condition of the items.

The following is an example:

Description Major	Exp. Life {Yrs}	% Depreciation Per/year Below Avg. Wear	Avg. Wear	Above Avg. Wear
Appliances Minor	12.5	5	8	15
Appliances Table	12.	5	8	16
Appliances Audio	9.3	7	10	21
Hard Furniture	18.3	8	12	23
Upholstered Furniture	12.2	3	8	10
Television/Video	10.3	5	9	15
Audio Equipment	10.3	6	9	10

Let us say we have a used sofa a client wants us to sell. They said their mother bought it about 10 years ago and paid $900 for it. Our chart says upholstered furniture has a life expectancy of 12.2 years. That means the sofa has 2.2 years to live. In addition, we give it 8% for avg. wear per year over 10 years that means 80% of $900=$720 of life expired. The value left is $900-$720—$180.

Let's look at another item, a 40" projection television set bought 8 years ago for $1000 and had 2 major repairs done on it. The chart says expired life is 10.3 years and average wear is 9% per year. 8 years x 9percentage x $1000 1720. The value of the television set is $1000-$720=$280.

Please note that hard furniture expected life is 18.3 years, almost 6 years over upholstered furniture. That would be tables, chests, cabinets and chairs all made of hard wood.

Antiques even though they are made of hard wood because antiques are appreciable items meaning they go up in value unless they are damaged and have new wood replacing any major element of an item, will render it undesirable.

Style, is a term used to denote apiece made in the manner of or fashion of an earlier period design but made later.

Over the years, we have sold a lot of antique furniture, some American and some European. Most of the later is English Sideboards made in 1850's to 1890's. Once in awhile you may have an older period piece to sell with its history or provenance. Make sure of its age, if necessary call in an antique appraiser to authenticate it. Then make it your lead item when you advertise for your next sale.

The chart on exhibit page uses monarch period to furniture period names. Styles of furniture found in homes and shops today are as follows:

Colonial or Pilgrim-c-Jacobean or William and Mary
1700-1760--------------Queen Anne
1750-1790------------Chippendale also referred to as Georgian by
English 1780-1815-------------Federal also Hepplewhite and Shearton
Hepplewhite legs are square and tapered as Shearton legs are rounded and may be turned. Shearton style is being used today, be careful in dating an item. Duncan Phyfe style has been mass-produced over the years using Shearton, Hepplewhite, Empire and Victorian designs or portions of them. 1815-1850---------Empire, Regency and Duncan Phyfe 1840-1900----------
Victorian also called Gothic (184018601860), Rococo (1845- 1875), Renaissance (1850-1880), Eastlake (18701900), and Cottage (1840-1900). 1890-1920---------Golden Oak, popular in its day, but like all popular things it is being reproduced in the orient. Art Nouveau was produced in Europe during this period but not in USA.
1905-1920----------Arts and Crafts also called Mission furniture. Famous makers were Elbert Hubbard and Gustav Stickley. Stickley is still being produced today. 1925-1945-------Art Deco. Days of the roaring 20's, beads and flapper dances. Then the great depression and WW2.
1945-1990-----Danish modem, Eames chairs, plastic, chairs covered with Naugahyde, Parsons Tables, wrought iron patio and porch furniture, French Provincial, American country.
1990- 2030--- Space Age furniture and styles from all over the globe. In furniture it has to be a fad, someone will take many styles like Poor old Duncan Phyfe did and become a hit in the international markets and we will have another style. So if you have the knowhow and ability go for it!

You can back fill with Amish type of furniture, Hitchcock style, and remember good furniture uses good material to make good stuff that will sell!

To know furniture, you must have a great knowledge of what it has made of like what kind of wood was used in all of the above styles.

Example: Styles Throughout The Ages

PERIODS & STYLES

Dates	British MoDa/Cb Period	British Period	FreDel Period	German Period	USA Period	Style	Woods
1558-1603	Elizabeth I	Elizabethan	RenaisSU			Gothic	Oak Period (to 1670)
1603-1625	James I	Jacobean		Renaissance	Early Colon...l		
1625-1649	Charles I	Carolean	Louis XI 1616-16-			Baroque (c1620-1700)	
1649-1660	Commith	Cromwellian	Louis XI 1643-17	Rellaissance			Walnut period (c1676-1715)
1660-1685	Charles II	Restoration		Baroque (c1650-1700)			
1685-1689	James II	Restoration			William & Mary		
1689-16/M	William & Mary	William & Mary			Dutch Colonial	Rococo (c1698-1760)	
1694-1701	WilliamIII	William III		Baroque (c1700-1730)	Qu""n Anne		
1702-1714	Anne	Queen Anne					Early mahogany period (d735-1770)
1714-1727	George I	Early Georgian	Regence (1714-172)	Rococo (c1730-760)	Chippendale tfiom 17601		
1727-1760	George II	Early Georgian	Louis XV 1723-177	Neo-classicam (c1760-1800)		Nei-classical (c1755-1805)	Late mahogany period (cf716-1810)
1760-1811	George III	Late Georgian	Louis XV (1774-179)		Early Federal (1796-1810)	Empire (c1799-1815)	
			Directoin (1793-179)	Empire (d800-1815)	American Direc Wire (1798-1804)		
			Empire (1799-1811)		American Empire (1804-1815)		
1812-1820	George III	~	Restauratk CharlesX 1815-183(	Raedenmeier (d818-1848)	Late Federal (1816-1830)	Regency (c18la-1830)	
1820-1830	George IV	Regency					
1830-1837	William IV	WilliamIV				Ecletic (c1836-1880)	
1837-1901	V"ICloria	V"IClorian	Louis Philip 1830-1841	RevsYale (d836-1880)	Victorian		
			2adEmpin Napaleon II (1848-1870)			Arts & CraftB (c1886-1900)	
			3rdRepubn (1871-1940)	Jugends1il (c1880-1920)			
1901-1910	EdwardVII	Edwardian			Art Nouveau (c1900-1920)	Art Nouveau (c1906-1920)	

When our girls go, through costume jewelry they check all gold for 14 karat or 18 karat also silver for sterling marks as well as things that look like Ivory and Jade. They set them aside for us to look at and determine if we need to have them tested. We have a diamond tester to checkout any large rhinestone. Not all that glitters is always gold and diamonds look good but may be a fake.

A quick test on Ivory is the red-hot needle in a spot that will not damage the piece. If the needle penetrates and sputters emitting a smell like burning feathers it is not ivory. A lot of fake carved ivory Netsukes have appeared on the market in the last 50 years. A Netsuke is an oriental three-dimensional piece from one to three inches high with a hole to attach them to a kimono.

Now jade testing can become more complex. First jade or jadeite is a very hard stone with a Mohs rating of 6.5 % compared to a diamond, which is the hardest with a Mohs scale of 10. Steel is rated at six 'h and will not scratch jade. Therefore, a simple test of scratching jade with the blade of a pocketknife is one method. A word of warning, if the item has been under very high heat or buried for a very long time, its specific gravity may have changed and more testing must be done. In addition, jadeite and nephrite may be mistaken for each other but nephrite has a hardness of six 'h and might be scratched.

You can buy a diamond tester from any jewelry supply house ours is a battery-powered tester, which is good in the field. RS MIZAR calls it Diamond Detective; it has a switch to test small stones or large stones. If it is a diamond, a small green light will flash on the diamond light it will also make a beeping sound to alert that it is a diamond. Warning, it will also test a Moissanite as being a diamond. They now have another tester that will test Moissanite. Cubic Zirconium (Zircon) tests like a piece of glass.

Rhine stones have become popular again, so do not throw out any jewelry that has some.

Cleaning costume jewelry is easy if you have the right equipment and cleaning solution. We have a small electric unit that will clean up to five rings at a time. Remember used costume jewelry means others and the oils wore it and body of the former owners will remain on the items.

So clean, before you examine the pieces of used jewelry and keep your hands clean. You can purchase a cleaner unit like ours or get a larger unit if you expect to receive a great amount of used jewelry.

Speed Brite Systems have a web site at www.speedbrite.com. Not only does it clean but also it brings out the luster of stones.

You can use this cleaner indoors at room temperature and creates no heat or sound waves.

It operates on an ionic process that simply bubbles in the Gem Sparkle solution. They also provide instructions for cleaning all types of stones.

You will be amazed at your customer's reaction to seeing your jewelry sparkling in your display cases.

Jewelry

Our jewelry section has grown considerably over the past 20 years. At one sale, my wife asked me to be the sales person taking care of the jewelry. She gave me a sales book, a pen, a calculator and a card table and oh yes a bag of already priced jewelry. I asked her what room was I to use for the jewelry sale. All the rooms are filled and I should set up by the swimming pool.

I found a spot in front of a large pillar where my back was protected. I spread out the jewelry and barely had room for my sales book.

They opened the doors and customers made a mad dash through the house looking for jewelry. They found me!

I spent the next 4 hours shouting don't back up or you will fall into the pool and no that stack belongs to him and I am writing her invoice for her *stuff*. No lady you have to pay here, you can't take it outside.

Another quick story that needs telling is about a lady just starting with us and was assigned to work in the jewelry room by herself. She sent a costumer to us saying she needed help. She had a costumer who wanted to see a necklace that was tangled up with other necklaces. It was a huge tangle about the size of a baseball. You probably have seen some like this and they are difficult to untangle. I was the person sent back to help her. I asked the buyer which one was the necklace she wanted to see and it was deep in the tangle. I offered to the buyer she could have the whole tangle for a few dollars, which she accepted. That sales girl became one of our best on jewelry but had to retire due to illness. We still miss her.

We have grown larger in the jewelry section from those early days and it has become one of the biggest sections of our estate sales. From one card, table to four long tables and several smaller tables, two sales persons, a cashier writing up the invoices. Of course, all those tables are holding up jewelry cases, and depending on the amount and value of the inventory determine how many cases are needed. Remember keep those cases out of direct sunlight because inside the cases the metal on the jewelry becomes very hot.

Most of the jewelry we get in estates are costume type, but be careful some of it may be antique.

There are several very good books on antique jewelry with suggested prices, which may be retail.

Pictures/Paintings/Prints & Serigraphs

Are all oil paintings good?

Not if they are forged or fake and meant to deceive you to believe it is an original. How do they do this? We are well into the age of computers and their ability to copy anything, even an old expensive oil painting. Computers can copy onto canvas and in exact color of the original painting. What it does not do is give the copy any brush strokes leaving highs and lows of the paint on the canvas. In other words, it will make a copy true in color but flat picture.

A very careful examination with good magnification will reveal a dot matrix in areas that have very little paint. The copier knows how to cover these areas with paint. To give the allusion of the original the copier will use a brush to paint over those areas that show brush strokes giving the copy the same feel if examined by hand.

Have we ever come across any such forgeries?

Yes on several occasions, one in particular, a University received a painting as a donation. It was a Harlequin painting by Picasso and signed by him.

The University asked us if we could authenticate it and put a value for their records. First, we found the original was half the size of the subject painting, secondly we found dot matrix under some of the paint. We concluded that it was a fake not a fraud because the donor was not asking for any money.

On another occasion we were doing an appraisal for a client who was very proud of a Remington painting he had purchased out West. It too had paint on top of a lot of dot matrix.

He was not pleased with our findings.

The point we are trying to make here is if you ever have any paintings that are painted over a copy. Do not try to sell it. When in doubt always consult with a qualified appraiser.

Not all pictures under glass are always a print; some may be a watercolor or a lithograph. Again, use a strong magnifying glass, a print will show a dot matrix pattern and a lithograph will show small lines. A watercolor will only have brush strokes and most always show a slight bleeding of colors on the edges. There are other pictures under glass that are none of the above and it is called a Serigraph. This is a screen printing process and it is not new, commercially used in Tee Shirts designs. In the

25

early 1960, Andy Warhol made it popular with his depiction of actress Marilyn Monroe. Today Le Roy Neiman, Peter Max and many more well-known artists are making serigraphs of their works and most of these are numbered copies and selling at good prices.

Example:

JADE

Three kinds of color but all jade

Pair Black Leather Arm Chairs; Sold for $900.00 Small <u>Table with Fossil; Sold</u> for $325

Art Deco Lamp and Pair of Suede Leather Arm Chair. Arm Chairs Sold for $600.00 Lamp

Lamp

Furniture

A Victorian Lady's and Gentleman's Chairs. Sold for $350.00.

Furniture

Mahogany English Break Front China Cabinet Buffet dated 1890-1910. Sold for $2,000.00

Furniture

English, Mahogany, Chippendale Style Table and eight Chippendale Style Chairs, dated 1850's, Sold for $1800.00

Furniture

A beautiful Tall Case Clock dated 1750's made in England, Sold for $8,800.00

Furniture

A beautiful Marble Top Credenza sold for $1,000.00

Furniture

A beautiful Edwardian Cabinet, sold for $450.00

Furniture

An Art Nouveau Boudoir Cabinet, sold for $450.00

Furniture

An Unusual Brass bed, sold for$650.00

Furniture

A Dressing Table Circa 1910-20's, sold for $575.00

A Large Pier Mirror, 8" 6" high, Victorian, circa 1840–1860 Price $2,000.00

Pair of Large Vases on bottom, European, circa 1900, 38" high, no mark Sold for $1,200.00

Arts & Craft Recliner Arm Chair, Oak, circa 1915 Sold for $250.00

Iranian Carpet, 8'2" x 6'3" Semi Antique Price $750.00

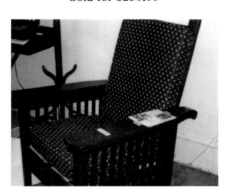

Mud men are becoming very collectable and can be found in upscale gift shops. Prices range from $20 to $50. Interesting where they originated and how they have evolved over the years. You can find them in most oriental pricing guides, listed under Shiwan Pottery. Shiwan Potters have been making pottery for over several thousand years. Shiwan is located on the Pearl River about 30 miles southwest of old Canton. They were not known for making expensive types of pottery and most items were considered rather clumsy made for kitchens. They have been known for unusual styles of glazes and some of their older pieces are sought after today because of their colorful glazes.

More recently, they are being known today for their mud men or figurines called Mud People. Many are copies of older pieces with adding more intense expressions on their bodies and faces. Older Mud People are hard to find and their prices range $300 to $500. A reproduction warning, as you know anything of great value will be copied and try to represent it as original. Most of these are different sizes.

A couple of good examples is on the following page and note the expressions on their faces and their body language.

Example:

Chinese Mud Men have become very collectable and be very careful because a lot of copies are made. Look for the stamp of CHINA in the clay on the back of the figurine. Below are two pictures of Mud Men.

Furniture: Sometimes we get unusual things like a mosaic table with a pair of Concrete <u>Dolphins to support the top</u>. It was sold for $700.00.

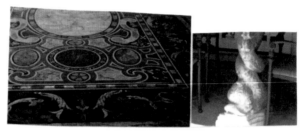

A large Abstract Painting measured 66 inches by 40 inches and sold for $450.00.

An Accent piece of contemporary furniture was this Fossil Stone Console, sold for $475.00.

Another unusual item was a Black Diamond Custom Pool Table. Sold for $2000.00.

CHAPTER 3

SETTING UP

Clean! Clean! Clean!

Setting up for an estate sale has a lot of work involved in cleaning up items that are to be sold and some that are not to be sold.

Let us assume you have a house that the Owners have left some things in and they are to be sold. There is a lot of room in the house for you to bring in other estates that may be in storage or will go directly into the sale house.

First step is to place identifying labels or tags with the "owner of the sale house's" code on all of the items left in the house. This is very important to do before any other estate's items are brought into the sale house. If not you may end up with some items that will be coded incorrectly and could cause you some serious problems when settling with your clients at the end of the sale.

Next step is to clean up the house, get rid of cobwebs and dirt. Dust all furniture, window ledges and shades, tops of television sets etc. Next setup a place for cleaning glass and porcelain items. Best way, if there is a dishwasher in the house, use it, will save you lots of time.

Clean out the garage, get rid of trash, broken items, old newspapers and magazines, clean the floor and work benches. If there are built in cabinets and shelves clean them out. Make sure the trash is put in trash bags and taken to the garbage pickup point at the street.

If you have card tables of your own, set them up in rows, leaving space between rows to walk between them. If you have any white sheets, putting them on the card tables will make them look better to display your items.

The garage at this time becomes your staging area for incoming boxes from other estates. Here you will unpack and tag all items with the proper estate's code and distribute them into the house or remain in the garage. Workers in the house will begin to bring items that would be better displayed and sold in the garage. Save some box lids to carry items in to house or to the garage.

Remember clean item's sell quicker than dirty ones. Keep a good supply of cleaning materials, clean rags, silver polish, furniture polish, dishwasher soap. A tip on cleaning silver, line a large pan with a layer of heavy-duty aluminum foil. Fill with a solution of very hot water and bicarbonate soda, the hotter the water and the more soda it will help clean the silver quicker. Our "Silver Queen" says you will find out yourself the right proportions of soda to water and how long to soak the silver. I think it's her trade secret, because when I ask her she says she experiments to get it just right It will take some elbow grease to use some silver polish and rags to get the final touch, keep those wore out tooth brushes to help get into those hard to get spots. It is necessary to have a good vacuum cleaner and some good sturdy brooms.

Silver Polishing

Some other stories make you laugh when someone mentions one of our sales. Like one day a girl cleaning silver by heating a double broiler on the stove.

Aluminum foil and water inside with baking soda. Several pieces of tarnished sterling silver tea and coffee service submerged in the liquid. She had turned the stove up as high as it would go; the double broiler was actually jumping up and down. We were concerned that the silver solder joints might melt. We turned the stove down and to our amazement the black tarnish had disappeared. Good job! However, do not try it.

The best method to polish silver using aluminum foil and baking soda (not to be confused with baking powder) is used in a large enameled pot, not to be used with aluminum or stainless steel pots. Do not line your sinks with foil as it may damage the sinks.

Bring the soda liquid to a boil, leaving the items submerged for at least 15 minutes. Using tongs to remove the silver items and wash them in soapy water. If the soda solution was not strong, enough some of the tarnish will not come off during the wash period. Our Silver Queen always says you have to experiment with the solution. After the items cool down you can begin to polish, we use (Wrights Polish) take one area at a time to make sure everything is working. Change polish rags frequently so not to put tarnish back on the items.

It's hard work to polish silver but you might experience a valuable find that I had at recent sale. Our Silver Queen was out of town, I had several items that needed cleaning, and I do all the pricing on silver anyway. One item was an Ice Bucket turned black with tarnish. After cleaning, I checked out the bottom for marks. One mark had a 925 in it, which denoted it was Sterling and on my scale, it weighed 42.5 troy ounces without its liner. Another mark was Italy and another was signed in script "Gino Marie Buccellati" who is one of the finest makers of sterling in the world. An ice bucket exactly like this one sold at auction in Geneva Switzerland, for $7,500.00 in 1999.

You have to cleanup and straighten up before setting up!

Silver and China on Dining Table. Use of Portable Shelves.

China

In your setup supply along with card tables, folding chairs, have some portable shelves. Many come in boxes and are easy to put together, about 36" wide by 12" deep and 6' high. Keep the boxes to put the shelves back in them for good storage after the sale. Place your shelves in good locations in the house, like the dining area if space permits. This is a good spot to display a set of dishes.

If there are clothes and linens to be sold, you will need to buy yourself a Tach-it gun and a good supply of attachment barbs to put your tags on the items. If you try to put stick on labels to cloth, it just will not work; they will fall off besides you do not want many priced labels lying around on the floor. You can order the Tach-it gun and barbs from Nebs, they are on the Internet, at nebs.com. You can order your sales books through them as well.

Normally it takes about one week to ten days to get your sale house organized and another week or two to get all the silver polished and priced. Again, the amount of time required will depend on how large a house and how many items you are putting in the sale. We have spent many a night catching up to meet our advertised sale date. Some nights we have actually seen people looking in windows (we assume they were buyers) with binoculars trying to read price tags and where items are in the house. Sterling silver always has the place of honor in our sales. It is always on the dining room table. Use a clean cloth to place your cleaned and polished silver. Sterling flatware in silver chests is placed on sideboards in the same room. We usually have one or two sales people at the Sterling silver, depending on how much silver we have for sale.

If we have a small amount of sterling, we will put the sterling on one end of the table and silver plate at the other end. We write up sales invoices on sterling at the table but do not collect any money; we hold the sterling at the table and give the buyer a copy of the invoice who will pay one of our cashiers and bring back the invoice marked paid to receive their purchase. This will be explained in detail in Chapter 8.

Persian carpets are a good seller, but it takes some care on where you place them in the sale house. Carpet on top of carpet never stays down and to keep the edges down you will have to use carpet tape (which is a two-sided tape). Here again the bottom carpet must be vacuumed clean or the sand and grit will adhere to the carpet tape and the carpet will come up. This will be a serious hazard for someone to trip on and fall. Yes, you had better have some good liability insurance; this will be explained chapter 6. Also, be careful on placing small Persian rugs on a well-polished wood floor, as it will slide causing a possible accident.

When we combine estates, we get many boxes. We also provide packers to pack up Dishes and what not items. As you see, they enjoy their work.

UNPACKING BOXES

<u>It is</u> a boring job and having company makes it better

SETTING UP THE GARAGE
Having lots of help makes the job more fun and getting it done!!

YA GOTTA EAT!

Sometimes the Silver Queen brings a homemade cake!

CHAPTER 4

COMBINE ESTATES

In doing a small sale where all of the items are in one estate or owner, you should not have any problems in accounting. The need to write a sales invoice is not necessary unless you might have to account for the sold price for each item.

Problems will occur when you have two or more estates or clients included in one sale. To help eliminate the problem of giving credit to the wrong estate/client and a need to account for items sold, you must have a method to keep the estate/clients separate.

In the previous chapter, we discussed setting up for a sale you want the house to look like someone is living there. Furniture placement is very important, for example, you should not place a sleeper sofa *in* the kitchen because it would not show as well. Often you may have several sofas in your sale and you would have them placed in the living and family rooms. In addition, items that would complement those sofas like end tables, lamps and smaller items. Now a problem becomes apparent, you may be mixing two or more estate items together.

In the previous chapter, we discussed tagging all items with a code and a price. We always start a sale with a code listing for all estates and keep the list current. When you have a large estate, some of the items may be carried over to another sale and keeping the same code used in a previous sale. When an estate is brought to final (all items are sold or returned), the code will be deleted from the list.

For the purpose of how this is, done we offer this example:

John Smith estate was a medium size from a two-bedroom condominium with the following items: 1 sofa, 2 recliner chairs, 2 twin beds, 1 queen size bed, 4 bedside tables, pots/pans, glassware, pictures and a number of small items. We would assign the code of JS for this estate and a tag with this code would be placed on all items large and small.

Catherine Brown estate was a small size, consisting of sterling flatware (8 piece setting for 12 places), holloware (coffee & tea service& miscellaneous bowls), jewelry (14 k diamond ring & costume pieces), 1 drop leaf table, and 6 table lamps. All of these items are tagged with the code CB.

The Sullivan estate was of medium size, consisting of a large screen projection color television set, 3 Persian carpets, king size bed, armoire, dresser with mirror, high boy chest, Chippendale style dining table with 8 chairs, 2 sofas and some miscellaneous items. Sullivan estate was assigned the code letter "S" for all of its items.

Another small estate was for a newlywed couple who had received several duplicates in their wedding gifts. A set of dishes and several appliances. Their names were Paul and Betty so their assigned code was "BP".

The trust department of a local bank wanted to close out an estate that had some pieces of good jewelry, and code of "B" was assigned to that account.

Another family had inherited a 12 place setting of Royal Daulton china with six serving pieces. A code of R" was assigned to the Roberts Family. We now have a "Code List" for six accounts as shown below:

JS ----------------- John Smith CB--Catherine Brown

S ------------------ Sullivan

PB ---------------- Paul & Betty

B ------------------ Bank

R ------------------ Roberts Family

Some of our larger sales could have as many as 28 codes or accounts. With this number of codes, it is very wise to tag all items with its proper code before putting them inside your sale house. If not, you might have a hard time later trying to remember who the owner of what was.

Once in a great while you might have a very large sale in a house with only one code and this makes accounting much easier.

The purpose of codes assigned to accounts has an extra benefit when you need to look back in your books and find the price of a sofa for the John Smith estate. In going through the invoice books for that sale; we found the JS code on a sofa that sold for $450.

Example of a Code List that shows more detail:

Code	Name	Address	City! State Telephone
JS	John Smith	1014 Circle Dr.	Any town (813)-825-6778
CB	Catherine Brown	547 E. 4th St.	My town (813)-665-2659
S	Sullivan	711 W. Lakeside Dr.	Your town (717) 243-7895
PB	Paul & Betty	2411 Apt. B., Honeymoon Dr.	Love City (312)-666-525
B	Your Safe Bank	1010 Money St.	Banking City (616) 323-6789
R	Roberts Family	1516 Heirs St.	Income City (234) 686-2543

Example Excel Work Sheet

	2	3	Excel Work Sheet
A			
B	BANK TRUST DEPT.		
C			
C	CATHERINE	BROWN	
B			
D			
E			
F			
G			
H			
J			
JS	JOHN SMITH		
K			
L			
M			
N			
O			
P			
PB	PAUL & BETIY		
Q			
R	ROBERTS FAMILY		
S	SULLIVAN		
T			
U			
V			
W			
X			
Y			
Z			

CHAPTER 5

ADVERTISING – MAILING LIST – POLICE

How will prospective buyers know that you are having an estate sale, where it will be and when it will be?

Yes, you will have to advertise on who, what, where and when. We call it the FOUR W'S for a successful sale.

Some of the various ways that you can advertise information to make a successful sale.

Have a mailing list of prospective buyers who are interested in not only where and when but actually, what you are selling and want to buy your items that are for sale. Where do I find such a list? Answer, you create it yourself.

The following is a time line of how to do this. At your first sale everything is priced and in place.

Prepare an advertisement for your local paper, neighborhood flyer, and local laundromats.

To be notified of the next sale, place a sign up table near the sale entrance inviting buyers to sign up, be sure you ask for name and mailing address.

You and your workers should always call peoples' attention to sign up. A simple question always works, "Are you on our mailing list to be notified of our next sale?" they will answer you like" I signed up or where do I sign up."

This is your best method to create your mailing list.

We have been doing estate sales for over thirty years and have a sign up table at every sale. It is amazing how quick the list will grow. You need to monitor this list to eliminate duplications and those who move away from your area.

Recently we decided to validate our list of names by asking on our mail out card that in order to stay on the mail out list that they bring this card to the sale. We had a box at the sign up table with a sign asking them to deposit there card to stay on the list. We ran this for three consecutive sales and purged our list, it was surprising, some had died, some had moved to another state and so on.

E-Mail using the internet is a lot cheaper if all of your buyers have a computer and know how to use it. We tried it once and found that people change their email address without telling you, which will cause your notice to be stopped. To overcome this you must confirm all e-mail addresses before sending out your sale notice.

If you have a couple thousand names, this will be *a* time consuming process. You can buy a soft ware program to handle this or stick with U.S. Mail.

Of course, both of these methods are good and useable, the main purpose is all who sign up for either list or both are potential buyers! The next step is preparing a notice of sale that can be placed on a post card. We have one of our notice post cards as an example (see on next page).

Another important part of having a mailing list is keeping a record of the names and addresses; we keep ours on a computer database. This database is in a computer.

In addition, it can be used for printing labels for your post cards. Next are having post cards that will be sent first class. We change the color of ours each sale and have a professional printer prepare the cards.

Why first class? After your list grows and grows and you have no way of removing names that have moved away, that is where first class helps; post office returns all first class cards that cannot be delivered. You might need a P.O. Box to receive these cards when your list get is up to a couple thousand names. In this way, you can police your list somewhat, and remember, if you are not sure your list is clean, you can put the notice of bring this card to next sale to stay on the list.

Whoa, Stop, Halt, wait just a minute, are you saying there is going to be that many cards? Yes there will be several hundred your first year and possible a thousand.

Wait, who is going to pay 29 cents a card or $290.00 per thousand? If you will, re- read the client's contract about advertising expenses. Ok, the charges are pro rated across all the clients who are selling stuff in this sale. This is the best way to advertise to your good quality buyers. Oh yes, we still advertise in the newspaper in the Estate Sales section, not in garage sales. We also put signs out the night before the sale.

Example First Class Post Card

Signs are expensive, usually costing about $50.00 apiece, so be careful where you put them or they will be gone the next day. (See example) We had put signs out a day ahead of the sale and we had to turn people away, some had beaten us back to the sale house.

Every sale requires a careful survey of the streets around the sale house and placing signs at busy intersections and directing them with the arrow to the sale house.

A word of caution before putting a sign on some one's yard, ask for permission to do so. I must confess I did not heed my advice and went to another sign stop and going back, I noticed my first sign was gone. Naturally, no one saw who took the sign! At $50.00 a pop, I became more careful and asked permission before putting the sign on someone's property.

Police are a great help and are needed as you get larger, traffic control is most important especially when people see a couple of hundred in line, they double park their cars and jump out to get in line. Yes, this is a true story; we were doing a sale in Largo, Fl., which was a multimillion-dollar estate. We had a 6-acre parking lot with signs and men directing cars to the lot. We had not open the doors yet and the line was over three hundred strong and growing every carload coming in, but not to our parking lot. They had double-parked on a two-lane dirt road over a half mile back to the main road. There were no side roads. Someone called in a complaint to the Largo Police Department that they could not get out because we had the dirt road blocked to the main road. About 30 minutes after the doors opened, we had about 75 to 80 customers in line at the sale cashiers to pay for their items. A motorcycle Policeman pulled into the cashiers' area and said we had blocked the road and he barely got through with his cycle. He said that he was shutting down the sale unless we removed the vehicles that were blocking the road. Otherwise he was calling wreckers to haul away cars. We called out all of our sales people to stand by all of the customers' items to be paid for so they could move their cars to the parking lot. At first, they did not want to leave their items. I saw a good customer coming down the driveway, I called out are they towing away any cars yet. He said one was hooked up and another one was getting ready to go. Those customers put down their purchases and ran to move their cars to our parking lot.

We had applied for off duty police two months in advance and were told we needed to apply one year in advance before we could be approved. The police had a helicopter circle over head and two patrol cars on the ground until the blocked road was clear.

We had five officers with us both days, pro bono. For those customers who were at that sale we thank you for helping us overcome that situation.

CHAPTER 6

CONTRACTS, COMMISSION, INSURANCE AND LIABILITY

Why contracts? We have two types of contracts, one for the owner of the house where we are conducting an estate sale. The other is for clients who are bringing things to the sale. Both contracts are to make sure there is a complete understanding between our clients and ourselves. Basically the contracts are really agreements and should explain the conditions that will help to have a great sale with no misunderstandings.

Why do you have two different kinds of contracts? The contract between the owner of the house where the sale is being held and us allows the owner certain advantages for the use of the house. We reduce the sales commission to 30% and have the house cleaned out after the sale is finished,

The contracts for clients who are bringing things to the sale are charged 35% commission. Both contracts explain how the cost for advertising is shared between all parties who have things in the estate sale. Both contracts state that all pricing of things in the sale are done by the company. The home owner's contract also agrees that the company is allowed to bring other clients personal property to the sale. This is a very important point, because if in the company's opinion the owner's property will not support a profitable sale or you might be told by the owner not to bring other items to the sale, as the owner does not want any competition for the sale of his property.

In cases where the house is very large and contains a lot of decent personal property, you might consider not bringing in outside property, but be very careful and very diligent in estimating the value of the owner's property. It has been our experience that the homeowner who wants this condition will also want an extra cut of your commission. Remember you are not in business to swap dollars or take a loss in the sale. In cases like this, you might explain your costs involved and offer to let him pay for off duty police for traffic control or pay for all the costs to prepare for the estate sale. If that does not work you would be better off if you refused to accept the job.

Included in this chapter are examples of the two types of our contracts we have been discussing. We are certain that these contracts will not meet everyone's needs or desires and your lawyer might recommend certain changes for your benefit, in fact our lawyer did make some changes to ours.

Insurance for liability is very important, if you need it and do not have it, it could be disastrous for your business. We shopped around and finally got the kind of coverage we need to protect the company and not hurt the homeowner who is allowing us to use his home for our sale.

There are many ways that you can help to eliminate personal injury to your buying clientele. We use a yellow and black adhesive tape to be placed on areas where step up or down can cause one to trip and fall. Stairs coming into the sale house and steps inside are necessary do places. You can purchase this type of tape at most Safety Supply wholesale places or they can direct you to someone who does sell this type of tape Remember, eliminate problem areas before they produce a lawsuit.

An example of putting you out of business actually happened to us, one of our workers was walking around looking for a place to hang a very nice picture and walking backwards, she fell into a hot tub. Fortunate the tub was full of water and the only thing hurt was her dignity and getting whenever we have a hot tub in the sale.

Now if a customer had fallen into that hot tub you would not be getting of as easy as wet clothes and a hurt dignity. Get smart, look for possible hazards both inside and outside of your sale house. Make your workers aware of the need to look for problem spots; you will be surprised how many places are just waiting for an accident to happen.

We sell a lot of costume jewelry and some good pieces now and then. Once we had an opportunity to sell a large amount of expensive jewelry, very nice pieces and even though we had a police officer with us, we had better check with our insurance company for some extended coverage. For just a couple of days the premium was more than we could make in a normal two-day sale. Sometimes, it is good to check on things like this before you commit and regret later. It is always prudent and safety minded but weighs the cost and advantages against the disadvantages. Having a police officer or deputy on duty at your sales is worth the expense and keeps the possible crime from happening. Disaster can happen and ruin your business; a true story of one estate Sale Company had their total of two days cash and checks in a brown paper bag setting on top of a cashier's table. Turned to tell something turned back the bag was gone. No police officer and no one saw who had taken the money. Crime is always looking for a place to happen.

Making good for all the items sold for two days plus paying all your help would be very hard to make up and continue in business.

These are not funny stories to make you laugh but a wakeup call to help you move up to the next *level from garage* sales or one client at a time type of estate sales.

ANY TOWN ESTATE SALES, INC.
P.O. Box 00000
ESTATE SALE AGREEMENT AT OWNER'S HOME

THIS AGREEMENT is made this   day of   20 ~ by and
between ANY TOWN ESTATE SALES and _____ - . J as owner or his
duly
appointed agent, personal representative or guardian (collectively"
Owner") of all the tangible personal property located at
_____ ----, (the Premises").

        WHEREAS, Owner, desires to engage ANY TOWN ESTATE
SALES. to
sell all of the tangible personal property currently located on the Premises,
except such property as described on Exhibit" A " attached hereto (the
Property") ; and
        WHEREAS, ANY TOWN ESTATE SALES, desires to accept
such engagement;
        NOW THEREFORE, the parties agree as follows:

        I.   Owner appoints ANY TOWN ESTATE SALES
as its exclusive agent to sell the Property pursuant to this Agreement.

        2.   ANY TOWN ESTATE SALES will inform Owner of the location,
dates and times, it will conduct an Estate Sale. All the property will be displayed
at the Estate Sale and will be marked for the sale at prices ANY ESTATE SALES.
deems reasonable.

        3.   ANY TOWN ESTATE SALES will retain percent (percentage) of
the
amount collected from property sales as compensation for services rendered
hereunder.

        4.   Owner agrees that all personal property currently located on the
Premises are subject to being sold except items specifically described on Exhibit" A
". If Owner refuses to make any Property available for sale after this Agreement,
Owner agrees to pay ANY TOWN ESTATE SALES percent (%) of the price at
which the Property could have been sold as reasonably determined by ANY TOWN
ESTATE SALES.

ESTATE SALES GUIDE

Chapter6

Contracts, Commission, Insurance and Liability

5. Owner agrees that ANY TOWN ESTATE SALES INC.
may bring other ITEMS of personal
property onto the Premises to be sold together with Owner's Property in a
combined Estate Sale if in the opinion of ANY TOWN ESTATE SALES, INC. the
Property alone will not support a profitable Estate Sale.

2.

ANY TOWN ESTATE SALES, INC. agrees to obtain from the owner of any other property
moved onto the Premises for the Estate Sale, a signed statement releasing the Owner from
any liability for loss sustained to such other property while located on the Premises.

6. Mailing list postage expenses and newspaper advertising expenses
relating to the Estate Sale will be divided among those parties whose property is being
sold in the Estate Sale in the proportion that the amount collected at the Estate Sale. All
moving, storage costs and minor furniture repairs, if needed, to be paid
by Owner. All packing done by ANY TOWN ESTATE SALES , INC. employees to be
paid by the Owner at $ per hour, per employee. ANY TOWN ESTATE SALES
INC. will deduct the portion of those expenses allocated to the Owner directly from
the Estate Sale proceeds.

7. Owner agrees to make the Premises available to ANY TOWN ESTATE
SALES INC. personnel at all reasonable times prior to the Estate Sale, not to
exceed   days, and further agrees to secure identical authority from any
new owner of the Premises if the Premises is sold during the term of this Agreement.

8. Owner agrees to continue to maintain all insurance coverages
necessary for all risks to the Owner's personal property and for the real property
where the personal property is located, with the exception of personal injury
liability which ANY TOWN ESTATE SALES INC. carries.

9. ANY TOWN ESTATE SALES " INC. assumes
no liability for loss to any
property which is not the result of its own negligence.

10. In the event it becomes necessary for ANY TOWN ESTATE SALES
INC.
to collect any of the amounts due under this Agreement through any attorney, by legal
proceedings or otherwise, Owner agrees to pay all costs of collection, including

ESTATE SALES, to collect any of the amounts **due** under this Agreement through any attorney by legal proceedings or otherwise, Owner agrees to pay all costs of collection, including the reasonable fees of any attorney (prior to litigation at trail and upon appeal).

IN WITNESS WHEREOF, the parties have executed This Agreement on the date above written.

ANY TOWN ESTATE SALES.   OWNER

BY_____   BY_____

ANY TOWN ESTATE SALES
AnyTown,USA
P.O. Box 0000

The reasonable fees of any attorney (prior to litigation at trail and upon appeal).

IN WITNESS WHEREOF, the parties have executed this Agreement on the date above written.

"OWNER"
By _____   By
                                              _____

By _____   BY

EXHIBITS "A"

The following is a list of personal property items on the Premises that the Owner desires to be excluded from the sale:

ANY TOWN ESTATE SALES
P.O. Box 0000
Any Town, USA

Exhibit "B"

The following is a list of personal property items that are not on the Premises and the, Owner will bring to the Estate Sale no later than ten (1 0) days before the sale date:

ESTATE SALE AGREEMENT FOR MERCHANDISE BROUGHT TO SALE SITE

This Agreement is made this _____ day of _____ , 200 ---" by and between ANY TOWN ESTATE SALES. and _____
_____ as owner or his duly appointed agent, personal representative or guardian (collectively" Owner") of all the tangible personal property consigned to ANY TOWN ESTATE SALES.

      1 . Owner appoints ANY TOWN ESTATE SALES as its exclusive agent to, sell the Property pursuant to this AGREEMENT.

      NOW THEREFORE, the parties agree as follows:

2.   ANY TOWN ESTATE SALES will inform Owner of the location, dates and times it will conduct an Estate Sale. All the property will be displayed at the Estate Sale and will be marked for the sale at prices ANY TOWN ESTATE SALES deems reasonable. ANY TOWN ESTATE SALES, will promptly dispose of all Property not sold at the Estate Sale to parties unrelated to ANY TOWN ESTATE SALES. at prices ANY TOWN ESTATE SALES, deems reasonable.

3.   ANY TOWN ESTATE SALES INC. will retain thirty percent (30%) of the amount collected from property sales as compensation for services rendered hereunder.

4. ANY TOWN ESTATE SALES, INC. assumes no liability for loss or damage to the Property while in its possession which is not the result of its own negligence. Owner agrees to hold ANY TOWN ESTATE SALES harmless for any damage to or loss suffered by the Property prior to its sale. In addition, Owner agrees to hold harmless any owner. lessor or lessee of the premises on which the Estate Sale occurs for any damage to or loss suffered by the Property. Owner will retain sufficient insurance coverage on the property during the term of this Agreement.

5. Mailing list postage expenses and newspaper advertising expenses relating to the Estate Sale will be divided among those parties whose property is being sold in the Estate Sale in the proportion that the amount collected from the sale of each party's property bears to the total amount collected at the Estate Sale. All moving, storage costs and minor furniture repairs, if needed, to be paid by the Owner. All packing done by ANY TOWN ESTATE SALE ˙ employees to be paid by the Owner at $ per hour, per employee. ANY TOWN ESTATE SALES will deduct the portion of those expenses allocated to the Owner direct from Estate Sale proceeds.

6. In the event it becomes necessary for ANY TOWN ESTATE SALES, to collect any of the amounts due under this Agreement through any attorney, legal proceedings or otherwise, Owner agrees to pay all costs of collection, including the reasonable fees of any attorney (prior to litigation at trail and upon appeal).

IN WITNESS WHEREOF the parties have executed this agreement on the date above written.

ANY TOWN ESTATE SALES,

"OWNER"

By_____
_____

By _____

CHAPTER 7

SALES PERSONNEL

The door opens and a buying hungry crowd rushes in, with one thing on their mind, getting something before anyone else gets it. Of course, they are looking for bargains, a lot of them are dealers or they may work for dealers. Some are looking for furniture to outfit a new home or a place in the mountains or at the beach for a second house. Others come to buy jewelry or second hand clothes. Some come just to see what is available.

We have a house rule that requires buyers not to pull price stickers off items without letting our sales personnel put their name on a sold sticker. We have sales personnel in every room and sometimes two if it is a larger room. On more than one occasion, some buyers pull price tags off items and carry them around to see if something else catches their fancy to buy. Usually someone else sees something without a price tag and gets one of our sales personnel to put another price sticker on the item. Guess what can happen and does happen, the person who pulled the first price sticker off goes to one of the cashiers and pays for the item. Someone else goes to our sales personnel in the room and has them put on a new price sticker and takes the second price sticker out to pay the cashier. Now who has bought the item? Others pull price stickers off things and carry them around then decide to throw the unwanted price stickers away. Either way it is against the company rules and makes for considerable arguments and fights between the customers.

Our sales personnel have another duty, if someone feels that a price is too high, the sale personnel offers them a bid card to place a bid on any item of $100 or more and the bid must be more than half of the price of the item. The cards are kept at the Silver table and sales personnel can check on the highest bid at any time and tell the bidder what he or she would have to go over. This bidding process quits at one o' clock pm on the second day and the highest bidder gets to purchase the item at their bid price.

Once a bidder is contacted and confirmed to purchase an item, we must put a sold sticker on that item immediately or someone might buy it paying full price, before we get the sold sticker on the item and it would be gone when the bidder came to pick up his item. This would present a king size problem for the company and our customers.

Sales personnel are not required to be knowledgeable about antiques or types and styles of furniture.

We do a walk through with all our sales personnel prior to a sale, giving them the pertinent information about all of the items in every room. Most of our people have a good knowledge about most things and stuff.

EXHIBITS

BID CARD

Item: _____ Code: _____

Price: _____ Bid Price: _____

Name: _____

Phone: _____

BID CARD

Item: _Wall Clock_____ Code: _JS_

Price: 5oo.oo Bid Price: _300.00_

Name: _Jack Dollar_

Phone: _555 - 5555_

CHAPTER 8

CASHIERS AND SALES BOOKS

Very important and valuable information about sales books and the invoices they contain. Each sales book has fifty (50) invoices and each invoice has twelve (12) lines. It is possible and many times happens that all twelve (12) lines have sold items recorded with the owner's code indicated on each *line*. This is very important so that all items sold for the owners can be tracked later if the owner wants to know how much a certain item sold for at the sale.

However, most important other than that above is the recording into the summary spread sheet that designates the amount of money to be distributed to all the owners.

We use a method of recording in a computer program called EXCELL. A soft ware program was developed with this program to handle a maximum of twenty books and with a minor change in the program; it could be expanded to handle twenty (20) additional books. The program will also accommodate fifty (50) owners' codes that sales are made on a commission basis. It will also handle ten (10) non- commission codes. Non commission codes may be used in various ways, for example, if the business buys up merchandise to close out an account or client because the estate must liquidate in a short time.

Another example would be where your employees would like to sell a few things of theirs and we allow this with a limit so that does not get out of hand or become a problem to the business.

The following example shows how our cashiers record the books and how this information is recorded into the computer program.

Some states may want estate sales to collect sales tax and the use of those columns in the example will have to be used accordingly. The use of the Non Commission section is up to the individual company as to how it is used but for company usage; it will prove very important if you buy up entire estates and placing those items for sale in one of your estate sales.

Each book in the computer program will have its own spreadsheet (which is exactly like the master or summary sheet) and the program combines all of the book sheets into one summary spreadsheet.

The Summary spreadsheet will show totals of each book and the totals under each owner's code. The summary will accommodate special charges under each owner's code such as moving expense, storage charges, packing charges, or other charges like advertising expense. The computer program divides all advertising charges equitable between all owners' codes by the amount of owner's sales compared to total sales.

In simpler terms, the owner whose sales are the greatest will pay a higher portion than the owner will whose sales are the least for the advertising expense. In addition, the prorated advertising expense can be extended into the non-commission sales area as well as the commission area. These are all programmed into the computer. They are found at the bottom of the summary spread sheet .Keeping a back up disc on each sale is very necessary if you have to reproduce a year before last to settle a dispute brought on by an irate heir or the sales tax inspector. Be sure to keep it in a very safe location.

The situation mentioned earlier is probably easier to explain now that you have a better understanding of sales books and spread sheets, simply put it is the method and procedure of not only getting your company's share of the sales profits, it also makes sure you know how much money you submit to the owners on the merchandise you have sold for them. It does sound simple right. Well suppose that after the sale is over, packing up your equipment is done, and you are setting up your computer to handle your latest owner's codes and preparing to transfer the sales books into the computer program, you find that some of your sales books are missing! UGH! You have only half of them. You search turning your car inside out, looking in every nook and cranny. I did not know there were any nooks and crannies' but I looked there anyway. Panic hit me like a ton of bricks, if I do not find those books how can I settle the owners' accounts? How much money should I give them? Who gets how much? With a cold knot in my stomach, I contemplated my options. Have you ever heard that trying to hide something you put it in something no one would look for? Well our cashiers save up those little plastic grocery bags and give them to customers to put their newly purchased items and carry out. Well setting on the floor of my office was a number of those little plastic grocery bags with various stuff and things in them. You guessed right, in that pile of bags were the missing sales books. Whew! Now we all know to handle those sales books like gold because that is what they are. It will never happen again! However, never say never, but do not let it happen to you.

How would you handle the problem if you did not find those books? I do not know and do not want to find out!

All of our cashiers have a great attitude toward customers and people in general. One of the more difficult jobs is our jewelry cashiers because they not only take the money but they are our sales person as well. It takes a lot of patience as well as a good knowledge of jewelry. They sell items as well as write up sales invoices and making change or taking checks. When the crowd gets large and everyone wants to get waited on and things get rather hectic. One of the best ways to handle this is to have a number system like in most large stores. This is why we say that our jewelry sales/cashiers are very special. Another type of sales/cashier is our Sterling Silver sales person. Our Sterling Silver is normally located in the Dining Room. With the Silver placed on the dining table and arranged for easy viewing. The sales person has a good knowledge of sterling silver, American as well as English silver, especially English hallmarks. European and Mexican Silver will often be discussed. When a sale is made, an invoice is made of the sold items. A copy of the invoice is given to the buyer and instructed to pay the outside cashiers and have the invoice copy marked paid. Return to the silver table and collect their items, which are held for them to be picked up.

This is an area where the situation gets critical when the volume of silver gets so large that we have to use two sales/cashiers at the silver table.

However, our jewelry and silver sales/cashiers are the most difficult positions and require the most delicate expertise.

Trying to serve a number of customers at the same time enhances the difficulty. In today's environment, everybody wants instant service. Usually this high volume of customers happens during the early hour of the sale. It is during this time that a number system is very helpful with crowd control.

Location of your jewelry display is very important. Good light is necessary but not in the sun because the jewelry gets too hot to hold. Inside where it has, air condition is best if you have room. However, do not hide it out back where it is difficult to find.

In addition, you will need display cases with glass tops for your expensive good jewelry. Costume jewelry can be displayed on top of tables. All items should have price tags on them. Having some knowledge of gems is good but not necessary for jewelry sales/cashiers. Our cashiers have many stories to tell but the best was the estate sale was at a large house on a one-lane road, we had a large lot about 5 acres in size. The owner had his yardman mow it for a parking. We placed signs directing where to park but customers parked on the sides of the one lane road and caused a traffic jam.

A Deputy Sheriff got through on a motorcycle and was going to shut down the estate sale if we did not get the cars into the parking lot. He wasn't kidding two Sheriff Helicopters were circling over head talking on their bull horns to cars to move are be towed away. At that time we had about 50 customers in line to be checked out and they didn't want to leave their stuff to move their cars. We brought all our sales people out and stood by their stuff while they moved their cars into the parking lot. That was an exciting time, we had Sheriff Deputies all over the place, and they bought stuff too. Where many people get together there is many stories to tell.

Where you put your cashiers is also very important, summer time always look for shady spots, winter time look for sunny spots, try to find spots where their backs are protected and customers can't get behind them, make sure they can always see the front door to watch for people coming out. We normally have between 5 and 7 cashiers during our sales, people will not wait long if they can't buy and leave.

Sales Book

NAME					DATE	
Mr. Money					01/01/01	

ADDRESS						
711 Big Bucks St.						
Rich City			PHONE	555-5555		

SOLD BY	CASH	C.O.D	CHARGE	ON ACCT.	MDSE. RET'D.

QTY.	DESCRIPTION	AMOUNT	
2	Paintings JS	500	00
3	Canton China S	150	00
		650	00

Tax # on file

" Tax no !

RECEIVED BY		TOTAL	650	00

41541 /Nims/ To Reorder: 800-225-6380 or nebs.com   Thank You

All claims and returned goods MUST be accompanied by this bill

Sales**Book**

Dates

From _____   To _____

Numbers

From _____   To _____

SPECIAL INSTRUCTIONS

Insert back cover flap under each set BEFORE writing
to avoid a carbon impression on the following forms.

All Sales Final

NAME					DATE	
ADDRESS						
				PHONE		
SOLD BY	CASH	C.O.D	CHARGE	ON ACCT.	MDSE. RET'D	

QTY.	DESCRIPTION	AMOUNT
	TAX	
RECEIVED BY	TOTAL	

41541 NEBS To Reorder: 800-225-6380 or nebs.com Thank You

All claims and returned goods MUST be accompanied by this bill.

CASHIERS
READY FOR CUSTOMERS

JEWELRY CASHIERS

WORKING WITH CUSTOMERS

CHAPTER 9

BOOKKEEPING, REMIT AND TAXES

After the sale is over and all items have been picked up, we need to make a list of the remaining items and their codes. We need this information to be able to advise our clients of what did not sell and we will take them to our next sale. See the example of "Remit Letter".

Before we send this letter, we need to know the client's bottom line or net profit from the sale. This information is found at the bottom of the summery sheet, which also shows cost of advertising, commission, expense, any moving packing, storage expense and net profit.

We have found most items that did not sell are those we call garage items and very often they would not sell if you pack them up for the next sale plus cost of packing, moving and storage would offset any profit. We always have a couple of "Flea Market Dealers" who will bid on these items. Some will offer to clean the house as part of their offer. That helps the owner of the house as they have put the house on the market.

A prompt "Remit Letter" helps to keep a happy client, and that is the best type of advertising. A long delay in sending the remit letter creates distrust and bad company/ client relations. One Estate Sale Dealer had a clause in his contract that stated he would not remit until all items had been sold. It seems that there were always one or more items never sold. He went out of business do to unable to work a sale from "Prison". I hope that anyone who has read this book doesn't get the bright idea to put that last item thing in a contract, because they might meet that guy who started it is in prison.

Going back to the list of items that did not sell, you might ask yourself why they did not sell. Was it priced too high or was this the wrong market for it? Was it damaged? Did you drop the price on the second day? Did someone put a sold sign on it but didn't buy it? T he last one could be a big problem for all estate sales companies. We tell customers coming in the front door that putting their sold stickers on items is not permitted. We have a sales person in every room that will do that for them. That is so we can get their name and telephone number, which is put on the sold sticker. We remember one sale that had about five different sold stickers on almost every item in the sale; some items had a couple sold stickers on it. After the rush was over many good, items had not sold.

What happened, some said they had changed their mind after they had put a sold on an item. It is bad enough when customers change their minds after they say there are going to buy. We take bids on our best items, one person had the high bid and I called the bidder who told me he changed his mind. He called me back and asked me if I would lower the price. I told him I was giving it to the next lower bidder. These things happen, so think about *why* some items did not sell.

To be successful in this business, treat your customer's right, be prompt in remitting to the owners, pay your help, pay your sales taxes on time and above all be honest all the time.

Good bookkeeping is also important, keep track of all expenses, little things add up and can keep you from having a great sale.

Sales Tax or Value Added Tax, if you do not know if you should collect tax you had better check with your state or country. Because you could be fined if you should collect and do not turn in any money. Worse yet you collect sales tax and do not turn in the money.

We know of one estate sales company who did not charge any sales tax over several years and was caught and fined several thousand dollars. So if you should be charging tax, get registered so you know how to keep from being fined. You must turn in a report even if one month you did not collect any tax. You can be fined if you do not turn in a report. Now this may vary by state or country.

As mentioned in chapter 8 regarding the spreadsheet it is a simple procedure of transfer of information from the invoices in the sales books to a record where you know a total of your sale, how much to your clients, how much goes to sales tax and how much you get to keep? This record in bookkeeping is called a Spread Sheet.

If you are having a small sale of say 6 clients and one of the clients is letting you use his house for the sale, we can use the same codes mentioned in earlier chapters and in our exhibit in the back of this chapter. If you do not have a computer or you are not computer savvy you can buy a pad of spread sheet paper at any office supply store and follow our instructions. At the top of your handwriting-spread sheet, you will notice that the paper is lined with columns and rows. Starting across the top the first column is for the invoice numbers in your sales book.

The next column is for tax exempt buyers (note exhibit in back) we put 1's to pay tax and O's for tax exempt (this is for our computer program) but you can use anything you want, just so you know if its tax exempt.

The next six columns will have your client's code in each one. These are the same codes on your tags of all the stuff and in your sales books.

Now across the top of the sheet over these codes write commission sales. Now go over a couple of columns and head a column with total commission sales. Now give yourself a couple columns for non-commission sales and mark that over the top of these columns. Next column you can write total sales and the next column mark it taxable sales. Next column write tax on top next column write calculated tax next column write total sales + tax next and last column write difference. At the bottom of the spreadsheet mark totals. If you: got lost, just go to the exhibit on book 1 and copy how it is laid out.

Now you are ready to go to work but first let me explain why you have a non-commission sale section.

You may have some stuff that you want to sell or people who work for you want to sell. We allow our workers to do this in limits not to exceed $100 dollars. If they exceed this limit, they drop out of none and become commission sales spread sheets.

By the way, if you use this method mark the top with Book 1 and so on because you will need them for the summary.

BOOK SUMMARY

BOOK #	JS	CB	S	PB	B	R				
1	50.00	10.00	30.00	150.00	90.00	20.00	0.00	0.00	0.00	0.00
2	0.00	0.00	0.00	0.00	0.00	0.00	0.00	0.00	0.00	0.00
3	0.00	0.00	0.00	0.00	0.00	0.00	0.00	0.00	0.00	0.00
4	0.00	0.00	0.00	0.00	0.00	0.00	0.00	0.00	0.00	0.00
5	0.00	0.00	0.00	0.00	0.00	0.00	0.00	0.00	0.00	0.00
6	0.00	0.00	0.00	0.00	0.00	0.00	0.00	0.00	0.00	0.00
7	0.00	0.00	0.00	0.00	0.00	0.00	0.00	0.00	0.00	0.00
8	0.00	0.00	0.00	0.00	0.00	0.00	0.00	0.00	0.00	0.00
9	0.00	0.00	0.00	0.00	0.00	0.00	0.00	0.00	0.00	0.00
10	0.00	0.00	0.00	0.00	0.00	0.00	0.00	0.00	0.00	0.00
11	0.00	0.00	0.00	0.00	0.00	0.00	0.00	0.00	0.00	0.00
12	0.00	0.00	0.00	0.00	0.00	0.00	0.00	0.00	0.00	0.00
13	0.00	0.00	0.00	0.00	0.00	0.00	0.00	0.00	0.00	0.00
14	0.00	0.00	0.00	0.00	0.00	0.00	0.00	0.00	0.00	0.00
15	0.00	0.00	0.00	0.00	0.00	0.00	0.00	0.00	0.00	0.00
16	0.00	0.00	0.00	0.00	0.00	0.00	0.00	0.00	0.00	0.00
17	0.00	0.00	0.00	0.00	0.00	0.00	0.00	0.00	0.00	0.00
18	0.00	0.00	0.00	0.00	0.00	0.00	0.00	0.00	0.00	0.00
19	0.00	0.00	0.00	0.00	0.00	0.00	0.00	0.00	0.00	0.00
20	0.00	0.00	0.00	0.00	0.00	0.00	0.00	0.00	0.00	0.00
TOTAL	50.00	10.00	30.00	150.00	90.00	30.00	0.00	0.00	0.00	0.00
COMMISSION	0.00	0.00	0.00	0.00	0.00	0.00	0.00	0.00	0.00	0.00
AD EXP	#DIV/0!	#DIV/0!	#DIV/0!	#DIV/0!	#DIV/0!	#DIV/0!	#DIV/0!	#DIV/0!	#DIV/0!	#DIV/0!
OTHER EXP										
MOVING	0.00	0.00	0.00	0.00	0.00	0.00	0.00	0.00	0.00	0.00
STORAGE	0.00	0.00	0.00	0.00	0.00	0.00	0.00	0.00	0.00	0.00
PACKING	0.00	0.00	0.00	0.00	0.00	0.00	0.00	0.00	0.00	0.00
OTHER										
NET PROFIT	#DIV/0!	#DIV/0!	#DIV/0!	#DIV/0!	#DIV/0!	#DIV/0!	#DIV/0!	#DIV/0!	#DIV/0!	#DIV/0!

COM SALES									TOT SALES	TAXABLE	TAX
35.00	0.00	0.00	0.00	0.00	0.00	0.00	0.00	0.00	35.00	35.00	35.00
0.00	0.00	0.00	0.00	0.00	0.00	0.00	0.00	0.00	0.00	0.00	0.00
0.00	0.00	0.00	0.00	0.00	0.00	0.00	0.00	0.00	0.00	0.00	0.00
0.00	0.00	0.00	0.00	0.00	0.00	0.00	0.00	0.00	0.00	0.00	0.00
0.00	0.00	0.00	0.00	0.00	0.00	0.00	0.00	0.00	0.00	0.00	0.00
0.00	0.00	0.00	0.00	0.00	0.00	0.00	0.00	0.00	0.00	0.00	0.00
0.00	0.00	0.00	0.00	0.00	0.00	0.00	0.00	0.00	0.00	0.00	0.00
0.00	0.00	0.00	0.00	0.00	0.00	0.00	0.00	0.00	0.00	0.00	0.00
0.00	0.00	0.00	0.00	0.00	0.00	0.00	0.00	0.00	0.00	0.00	0.00
0.00	0.00	0.00	0.00	0.00	0.00	0.00	0.00	0.00	0.00	0.00	0.00
0.00	0.00	0.00	0.00	0.00	0.00	0.00	0.00	0.00	0.00	0.00	0.00
0.00	0.00	0.00	0.00	0.00	0.00	0.00	0.00	0.00	0.00	0.00	0.00
35.00	0.00	0.00	0.00	0.00	0.00	0.00	0.00	0.00	0.00	0.00	36.00
0.00											

CAL TAX	TOT W/TAX	DIFF	ADJ TOT	BOOK #
35.00	35.00	0.00	0.00	1
0.00	0.00	0.00	0.00	2
0.00	0.00	0.00	0.00	3
0.00	0.00	0.00	0.00	4
0.00	0.00	0.00	0.00	5
0.00	0.00	0.00	0.00	6
0.00	0.00	0.00	0.00	7
0.00	0.00	0.00	0.00	8
0.00	0.00	0.00	0.00	9
0.00	0.00	0.00	0.00	10
0.00	0.00	0.00	0.00	11
0.00	0.00	0.00	0.00	12
0.00	0.00	0.00	0.00	13
0.00	0.00	0.00	0.00	14
0.00	0.00	0.00	0.00	15
0.00	0.00	0.00	0.00	16
0.00	0.00	0.00	0.00	17
0.00	0.00	0.00	0.00	18
0.00	0.00	0.00	0.00	19
0.00	0.00	0.00	0.00	20
3,500	3,500	0.00	0	TOTAL
	DEPOSIT	DEPOSIT		COMMISSION
				AD EXP
				OTHER EXP
				MOVING
				STORAGE
				PACKING
				OTHER
				NET PROFIT

EXHIBIT

January23,2001
Ms. I. M. Riches Any
Town, USA 33333

Dear Ms. or Mr. Riches

The statement on the sale conducted at, 3535 Money St. Any Town, USA, on January 14 &
15, 2001, is as follows:

Gross Sales $ 437.00
Less Commission $ 109.38
Less Advertising   10.25
Less Moving   000.00
Less Packing   000.00
Less Other   000.00
Net Profit $ 317.87

Enclosed please find a check for the amount due you. Items, that did not sell in this
sale, will be placed in a future sale. The following is a list of remaining items:

One Oil Painting
 Shirley Temple Doll
 Karastan Carpet

We appreciate your allowing us to handle this for you. If we can be of further service
or assistance, please call us.

Sincerely,

CHAPTER 10

APPRAISAL SERVICES

As you become more knowledgeable about pricing residential contents, you may be able to provide appraisals for estate values on division of property or tax purposes.

Preparing an appraisal that will be acceptable in the Courts and answer the questions that will challenge your ability to provide the information in any appraisal. An area that will be challenged is your resume' on experience and education as to knowledge of antiques and collectables.

To enhance your résumé', look for schools and courses on learning values of antiques and collectables. Check out places like museums that offer courses. Some may be on fakes and fraud, or societies who offer courses on pricing. These maybe expensive but very valuable when you add them to your qualifications.

The appraisal field includes not only estate appraisals but also divorce appraisals and donations that use the Fair Market Value rule. Usually most of these are on residential contents.

Many appraisers avoid Divorce appraisals because most the time you will have to appear in court to defend your appraisal values as well as to your qualifications.

An appraisal cover document is necessary to explain how you arrive at your values and what interest you have, if any, as to acquiring any of the items listed in the body of the appraisal. Lawyers will question you if any of the parties in the divorce are related to you and has anyone asked you to make values that will influence the outcome of the case.

Other types of appraisals are for Insurance and Bankruptcy, which require a different value than Fair Market Value.

The Insurance appraisal the values are for replacement, which could be retail or cost to make an exact duplicate of the items being insured.

The Bankruptcy appraisals are usually pennies on the dollar and a forced liquidation. Here again to be asked to make one of these you will be asked by the courts and your qualifications must be good.

The appraisal work provides a natural relationship to your estate sales business. You may be asked to appraise items that you never have in any of your sales. We have had some valuable paintings to appraise and have called in some experts in certain fields that have excellent qualifications. A strong word of advice and caution, before you accept an appraisal assignment, go look at the items and if you are not qualified to arrive at proper values turn the job down. Of course if you have some experts in the necessary fields that could help.

The best way to find these experts is by joining one of the Appraisal Societies. All have excellent ways of networking to help each other. Some have local Chapters that enlarge your field of help by being closer to you and your work. Some you will find are doing estate sales too.

This book is not intended to make you an appraiser but to give you another method of enhancing your income.

ABOUT THE AUTHOR

Angell Estate Sales & Appraisal Services, Inc.

Accredited Member of International Society of Appraisers

P O Box 1461
Brandon , Florida 33509-1461

Margaret Angell-Evans
W Diehl Evans
(813) 685-3477
(813) 689-1894 Fax

Professional Profile
For
W Diehl Evans

Academic Background

Accredited Member International Society of Appraisers

Sotheby's Institute on Ceramics

Sotheby's Institute on Fine Arts & Furniture

Winterthur Museum on Evolution of Style & Restoring Antiques

Museum of Southern Decorative Arts (MESDA) on Fakes & Frauds

International Studies- France, University of Caen, Fine Arts
and Architecture, with field trips in Normandy, Brittany and Paris.

Professional Background

Dealer in American, European, Oriental Antiques & Collectibles 1972-1985

Show Dealer in American, European And Oriental Antiques 1985-1990

Vice President Angell Estate Sales& Appraisal Services 1995-2010

Licensed Florida Real Estate Broker 1985-2010

Selected Clients

Band of America- Trust Department
Sun Trust Bank Trust Department
Northern Trust Bank Trust Department
Nancy Harris Esq. and Assoc. Attorney's at law

Membership

Accredited Member International Society of Appraisers
Past President of Kiwanis Club Of Greater Brandon, Fl.

CPSIA information can be obtained
at www.ICGtesting.com
Printed in the USA
BVXC01n0410131114
374747BV00001B/8